AVIATION PHOTO ALBUM 2

S0-BLO-362

AVIATION PHOTO ALBUM 2

compiled and edited by
MICHAEL JF BOWYER

PSL Patrick Stephens, Cambridge

© Patrick Stephens Limited 1980
All rights reserved. No part of this publication
may be reproduced, stored in a retrieval system
or transmitted, in any form or by any means,
electronic, mechanical, photocopying, recording
or otherwise, without prior permission in writing
from Patrick Stephens Limited.

First published — 1980

British Library Cataloguing in Publication Data

Aviation photo album, 2.
  Aeronautics — History — Pictorial works
  I. Bowyer, Michael John Frederick
  629.133'09'04   TL515

  ISBN 0 85059 410 3

Text set in 9 on 10pt Helvetica
by Industrial Artists (Hitchin) Limited,
Hitchin, Herts.
Printed in Great Britain on 100gsm Pedigree
coated cartridge and bound by The Garden City
Press, Letchworth, Herts, for the publishers,
Patrick Stephens Limited, Bar Hill, Cambridge,
CB3 8EL, England.

CONTENTS

INTRODUCTION

March 1978 saw the publication of *Aviation Photo Album.* It proved very popular, so much so that in answer to many requests more material remaining from the *Airfix Magazine* Photopage feature of years passed has been brought together in this second photo album.

Aviation Photo Album arose from a desire to present in one volume as many as possible of the photographs which had been submitted for *Airfix Magazine*, but for which there was never sufficient space. This volume carries photographs held over from the first volume. Our feeling was that rather than introduce one costly volume it would be better to bring out lower priced albums which would be more within the pocket of young enthusiasts who so very clearly enjoy the sort of material presented.

Again, the photographs span the whole period of aviation history from pre-World War 1 to aircraft of much more recent years. There is no doubt that the most popular section of the first volume was that devoted to aircraft of World War 2 and its immediate aftermath. Thus, we have devoted a major part of the book to this period. Nevertheless the other sections carry some rare material, much of it hitherto unprinted.

Captioning has again been kept to a minimum for the photographs are the main feature of the book. Some readers of the first volume considered that captioning might have included more detail and in this volume the captions are in some cases longer — where this does not reduce the size of the photograph.

We have made every attempt to contact each contributor of photographs, as was the case with the first *Photo Album.* In some cases it has proven impossible because photographs were submitted without contributors enclosing a name and address. Our thanks must go to the many who have been prepared to lend us photographs, many rare and on loan for a considerable time. If you are one of the contributors who we were unable to contact please write to us now.

Quite clearly, volumes of this nature are very popular. That being so, if you have photographs which you think would have wide appeal, please contact us.

Happy viewing!

Michael J. F. Bowyer

Michael J. F. Bowyer
Cambridge, November 1979

Right As a note on the original print summed up the situation — 'The bloke wot 'it the chimbley — or a spot of bother aboard the *Glorious*'. No 812 Squadron boarded HMS *Glorious* for the Mediterranean in August 1935, and this accident happened off Alexandria the following November. S1662, built as a Ripon II, had been converted into a Baffin by the time the photograph was taken *(R.A.Shaw).*

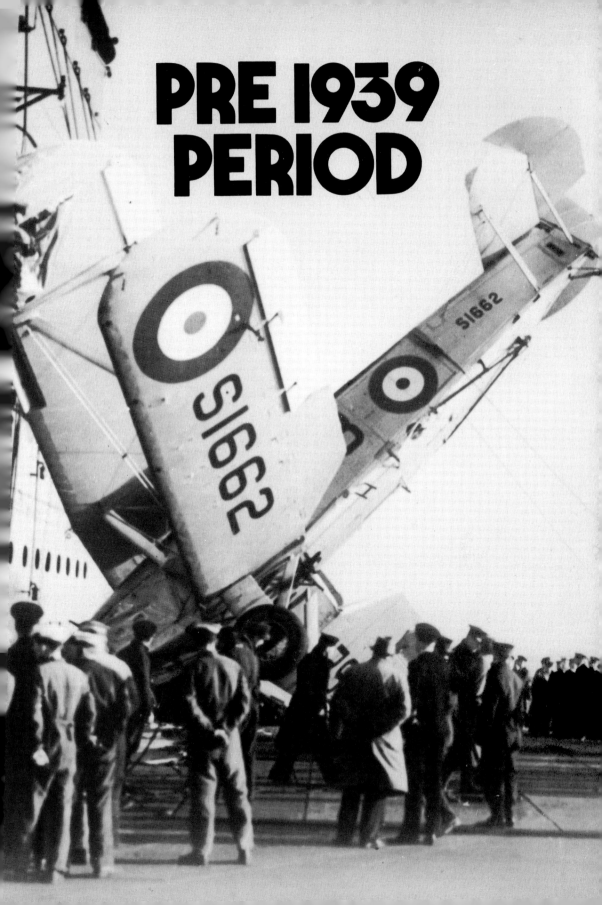

PRE 1939 PERIOD

Above The Coastal C7 airship which was stationed at East Fortune and Longside (R.Daniels).

Left Napier-built RE 8 A3871 served with No 3 Squadron, Australian Flying Corps (W.D.Brookman).

Left Apart from the fact that it is a Fokker DVII no more information is available (W.D.Brookman).

Above Superb definition characterises this shot of a Henry Farman biplane, circa 1910 *(John Hocken)*.

Right This DH 9A, F1036, served in No 110 Squadron. It was built by Westland. An SE 5A is in the background *(W.D.Brookman)*.

Right Look what we've found now the ice age has passed! A Sopwith Camel B5167 in No 28 Squadron markings *(W.D.Brookman)*.

Above A very smart DH 9A, E8754. The aircraft was used by the late Marshal of the Royal Air Force Sir John Salmond, and was photographed in Iraq in 1924 *(M. Schoeman)*.

Left No serial number is available for this Sopwith 1½ Strutter of No 5 Wing, RNAS *(M.Kent)*.

Below left Blackburn Ripon II 'No 14' of 466 Torpedo-Bomber Flight crosses the stern of an aircraft carrier in this 1932 photograph. No 466 TB Flight joined No 465 to form 811 Squadron on April 3 1933 *(R.J. McClachlan)*.

Above right Only one Bristol 99 Badminton was built, G-EBMK. It flew in May 1926, and took part in that year's King's Cup Air Race, force landing near Oxford with fuel flow trouble. At that time the engine cylinder head helmets, visible on the photograph, had not been fitted *(R.Morgan)*.

Right Beardmore WBIII N6115 poses, wings folded, by the mighty guns of HMS *Renown*. The aircraft attempted to fly off the fo'c's'le of the battle cruiser in 1917. Later, *Renown* had a turret ramp fitted *(R.Daniels)*.

Above Only one Gloster Gannet ultra-light sporting biplane was built, G-EBHU. It flew in October 1923. Later, a two-cylinder Blackburn Tomtit engine was fitted. G-EBHU is illustrated here in that state. Wing span was only 18 ft, length 16 ft 6 in, and loaded weight 460 lb. Top speed was 72 mph *(Don Gibbard)*.

Below I wonder how many people would nowadays volunteer to join these sailors manhandling a Ripon II like '61' seen here aboard HMS *Glorious*? *(N.Leicester)*.

Above A quartet of Wapitis. J9720, nearest, appears to wear a red fuselage band like the others which include J9399 and K2262 'L', the latter being a Wapiti Mk VI dual control trainer. All appear to have matt black fuselage upper decking and interplane struts *(A. Morris)*.

Below Hawker Horsley J7997, one of the few Mk 1s built. The Horsley served as bomber and torpedo bomber. No details of the accident shown here are to hand *(A.Morris)*.

Above If only someone had kept just one! What a magnificent sight, Handley-Page HP 42 'Hadrian' of Imperial Airways in the floodlights at Aboukir in February 1936 *(R.A.Shaw)*.

Below Not the ideal three-point landing — 'two wheels and a prop' — is what KR-1702 is suffering from. Built as a Fairey IIIF Mk IVB, the aircraft was converted into a Gordon in 1934. The photograph is reputed to have been taken at Aboukir in January 1935 *(R.A.Shaw)*.

Above No details of ownership are known for this Fairey IIIF Mk III, S1805, which comes from the final batch of serials in the 'S' range. Finish is standard silver with probably matt black decking and struts *(N.Leicester)*.

Below Another from the last of the Ss, this Fairey IIIF Mk III floatplane, S1834, comes from within the batch S1779-1865. This example appears to have dark green fuselage decking and struts, including those which attach the floats to the fuselage *(R.W.Elliott)*.

Background photograph Gone — almost — with the wind. Khormaksar, Aden, in March 1939 after a violent sandstorm had left three of 8 Squadron's Vickers Vincents looking worse for wear. K4128 nearest appears to have 'H' ahead of the fuselage roundel in yellow outlined black. K4143:J and K4663 are also in bad health *(G.Burn).*

Inset The only Vincent with wing warping? No, K4143 after the Khormaksar storm. The sand bags are there to stop the aircraft blowing over in a gale . . . *(G.Burn).*

Above It seems 55 Squadron has long been in the refuelling business, but filling the tanks of this squadron Vincent, K6326, is a far cry from messing about with Victors *(R.Kirby)*.

Below In its element, Vincent K6336 bearing 55 Squadron's badge on its fin. The spats each appear to carry a red flash. This Vincent was one handed over to the RNZAF in October 1939 *(R.Kirby)*.

Above S1464, a Supermarine Southampton II used by 201 Squadron. No details of where or when the photograph was taken are known *(R.W.Elliott)*.

Below There was a time when Fairey IIIF floatplanes were as native to the Nile as crocodiles. Both shown here are Mk IVMs, J9064 with J9060 to the rear. It is a fair guess they are of 47 Squadron *(M.Schoeman)*.

Left Luckily I had the camera with me, and this Ripon just comes alongside and I shot it. S1559 in the photograph was, at the time, with 466 Flight *(R.J.McClachlan).*

Below left Sutton Bridge in 1935 with Fairey Gordon K2728 outside a hangar used by the local unit, No 3 Armament Training Camp. Used as a target tower, the silver painted machine crashed in April 1937. It has underwing serials, and probably carried no unit markings *(R.Kirby).*

Below A companion for K2728 at Sutton Bridge, Bulldog IIAs of 17 Squadron during their 1935 summer camp. K-2491, later used by No 3 Squadron, wears the customary anti-dazzle top fuselage marking, probably black in this case as was usual on 17 Squadron's machines *(R.Kirby).*

Right All the panache of the 1930s. Fortunately it is still possible to hear the sound a Gauntlet made, albeit from Shuttleworth's Gladiator. The Gauntlet II here, K5359, wears 17 Squadron's markings and has black fuselage decking which was unusual on Gauntlets. The aircraft was written off when it made a crash landing at Kenley on May 8 1937 *(E.Nicholls).*

Below right No, they aren't models although they look like it. These are genuine Singapore IIIs basking in anonymity *(R.Kirby).*

Below A far cry from 24 Squadron's hefty Hercules of today, a Hawker Hart (Communications), K3874. On its silver finish '24' appears in black. In the background is a most interesting Magister, L5931, which has red flashes on its spats *(R.W.Elliott).*

Above Getting ready for a display at Old Warden? No, sorry to disappoint you. These three Vildebeests of the Royal New Zealand Air Force, NZ103, NZ102 and NZ111, are over their homeland *(N.Leicester)*.

Above left A line-up of Hart 1s at the Air Armament School, Eastchurch, circa 1935-36. K2472 has had its cowling overpainted silver whereas some others remain polished. K2472 reached Eastchurch in May 1933 and stayed until February 1939. Shortly afterwards it was despatched to the South African Air Force *(R.Kirby)*.

Left Nostalgia! Three Armstrong Whitworth Ensigns, a DH 86 and an HP 42 at Croydon *(R.R.Prior)*.

Above Many would expect a modern-looking stream-lined aeroplane to be made of metal, whereas one is apt to think of wooden aero-planes as a collection of struts and string. Not so, as this shot of DH 91 Alba-tross G-AEDL 'Fingal' at Croydon in 1939 shows *(R.R.Prior)*.

Right What's so special here? Yes, the Leyland truck '5168' is towing a Hawker Demon, at Hal Far. The Demon in camouflage finish had been brought by sea during the 1935 Abys-sinian crisis. What makes it rare is that the aircraft belongs to 74 Squadron. Their Demons in all their glory seem to have com-pletely evaded the camera *(M.Schoeman)*.

Above Go on, guess its squadron! Yes, we all know it's a Hawker Hind, but the squadron? Surprisingly, .No 112. Previously K6824 had served with 82 then 113 Squadrons before ending up in Egypt with No 112. It crashed when taking off from an Egyptian airfield in August 1939 *(D.Robinson)*.

Below Harvard 1 N7003 in its pre-war all-yellow finish. This was the RAF's fourth Harvard, and it joined 12 FTS on January 10 1939, passing to 14 FTS at the end of August 1939. It was in their hands when it was destroyed in a crash in Bedfordshire in May 1940 *(R.W.Elliott)*.

Above Swordfish 1s flying from HMS *Ark Royal* just before the 1939-45 war. L2720 certainly has colourful markings which appear to consist of two red and a central blue diagonal band and a blue fuselage band, all on a silver finish. '680' has been applied in white. L9780 seems to have a blue band across its fin *(T.Bowater)*.

Below Photographs of Hart variants in use as trainers are surprisingly scarce. K4425 seen here in yellow finish with polished bare metal cowling carries '13' in black ahead of the roundel. A Hart (Special), it joined 7 FTS in April 1936 and continued with the unit into the war *(G.Burn)*.

Above Fighters of the 1930s, Avia 34s of the Czech Air Force. Beneath that white square on the fuselage side is in each case a small four-digit black serial number such as B.5343. Finish appears to be dark green — overall? *(V.Jelink).*

Below As the song goes, 'Isn't she lovely, isn't she beautiful?' DH 86 L7596 was G-ADYJ before she was purchased for the RAF and used by 24 Squadron until destroyed in a crash at Ulverston, Lancs, in July, 1939. Note the underwing serials on the silver finish *(R.W.Elliott).*

Above 'When all at once I saw a Cloud,' a strange looking creature, with engines loud placed high, aloft. K3729 was photographed whilst with the Air Observer School at Manston *(B.T.Gibbins)*.

Below A Battle in the usual Dark Green-Dark Earth-Night finish of pre-war days, but unusual in that it was in the hands of the Special Duty Flight, Aeroplane & Armament Experimental Establishment, from September 1937 to November 1940. After storage at 32 MU it joined 16 Squadron in June 1942, staying with that unit until January 1943. It was struck off charge on June 30 1943 *(R.W.Elliott)*.

Above 'I was walking on the sands, your honour, when suddenly this great dragonlike machine came charging towards me. I took its number, G-ACNJ, and made the pilot stop. He admitted he was flying a de Havilland DH 84 Dragon II of Jersey Airways, and that it was 1935' *(Alan Murphy).*

Below If you cannot recall the late 1930s then you may not quite realise the impact which the DC-2 had upon the transport scene. Yet PH-ALI, a DC-2, might pass for a 1979 Dakota, which would look quite at home on any international airport apron. That shows how advanced the aircraft was in the mid-1930s. PH-ALI is at Habbaniya when Baghdad Airport was out of use in the winter of 1938/39 *(R.Kirby).*

Above Britain's answer to the racy Avia 34 — the Hawker Fury II. The Fury was a high-speed interceptor fighter for defence of special targets. The spatted Mk II seen here was a rare, exotic creature. K7281 is shown in 41 Squadron's hands, and was photographed on October 13 1938 *(C.Sanders)*.

Below Soon such biplanes had gone, along with their bright colours, as witness this Northolt scene with TM-coded Hurricane 1s on the apron in early 1939. The under surfaces are black and white, and the code letters were a shade of pale blue — not the medium grey some would have us imagine. The pre-war Frog Penguin kits carried transfers of the code letters which, at the time, could be seen to be fairly authentic *(D.P.Dunn)*.

These flying boats of the RCAF are PBY-5A Canso amphibians. 'Y' leading is 11063, R 11009 and D 9636. They appear to be white overall, and all have fuselage and wing ASV aerials *(K.Morris)*.

1939-45 PERIOD

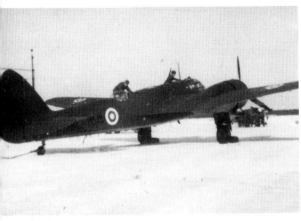

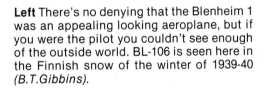

Above A very rare shot indeed. Just to see if it was as good as rumoured, the RAF borrowed a Curtiss Hawk H-75-C1, No 188, from the French Air Force, in December 1939. Here it is at Tangmere before commencing comparison trials with British fighters at Farnborough and Boscombe Down *(R.Staton)*.

Left There's no denying that the Blenheim 1 was an appealing looking aeroplane, but if you were the pilot you couldn't see enough of the outside world. BL-106 is seen here in the Finnish snow of the winter of 1939-40 *(B.T.Gibbins)*.

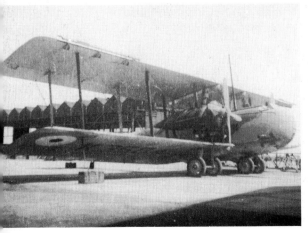

Left In the Middle East, and particularly before the war, the Vickers Valentia gave fine service as a long distance transport. K3604 is shown here at Khormaksar where, in 1940, it was in the hands of the Aden Communications Flight. The upper surfaces are camouflaged, probably Dark Green and Dark Earth, but were the under surfaces still silver? The aircraft was struck off charge in March 1941. Incredibly, these slow, lumbering giants were used for some night bombing raids against desert targets in north Africa *(G. Burn)*.

Right What use the Germans made of
French aircraft which they captured in 1940
seems not to have been much recorded.
Shown here is one such prize, in German
hands at Abbeville *(A.R.Chapman).*

Below The replacement of the Valentia was
the Bristol Bombay, one of which is seen
here in 1942 bearing the white disc and red
cross marking of an ambulance aircraft
(contributor not named).

Above Surely the Finnish Air Force was engineered for the benefit of Finnish aviation enthusiasts? Little wonder it remains such a fascinating organisation. Seen here is a Junkers Ju 34, JU-133 *(B.T.Gibbins)*.

Below As well as Blenheim 1s, the Finns also used Mk IVs like BL-197 seen here from the batch BL196-205 *(B.T.Gibbins)*.

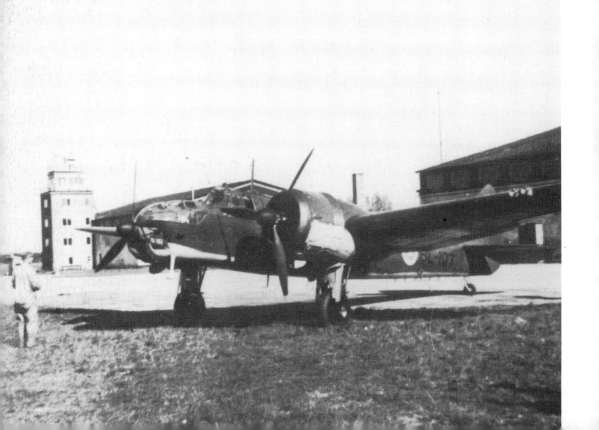

Above Taylorcraft Model Plus C G-AFUY in an unusual pose. It received its Certificate of Airworthiness in July 1939 and was based in Derbyshire. The aircraft was impressed in July 1941 — at which time the photograph was taken — and became ES957. After use by 651 Squadron it crashed at Tilshead in December 1941 *(W.D.Brookman)*.

Below A close-up of the nose of G-AFUY. The finish of the aircraft was Dark Green and Dark Earth with yellow under surfaces *(W.D.Brookman)*.

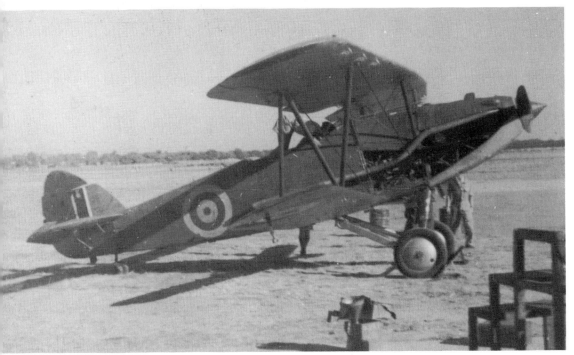

Above Wartime photgraphs of Audaxes are rare. This example was photographed at New Delhi, and wears a mixture of national identity markings suggesting a 1942 photograph *(G.Hicks)*.

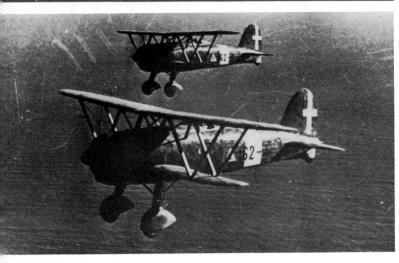

Above left A considerable number of Tiger Moths passed through the Taylorcraft works at Rearsby during the war. One can be seen here in a rare photograph from W.D.Brookman.

Below left Likely adversaries for the Gladiator, Fiat CR 42s of the 162nd Squadron, Regia Aeronautica *(Peter Sutton)*.

Above Gladiator XO-S: K7893 photographed in Egypt. It was a Mk 1 with a long and varied history. It first served with 3 Squadron and then with Nos 73, 3, 72, 80 and 112 Squadrons (in whose hands it is seen), then 3 (RAAF) Squadron and finally with 1411 Flight with whom it was serving when lost on July 20 1942 (D.Robinson).

Right Another Fiat CR 42, this time of the 95th Squadron and said to have been photographed in 1943 (M.J.Allen).

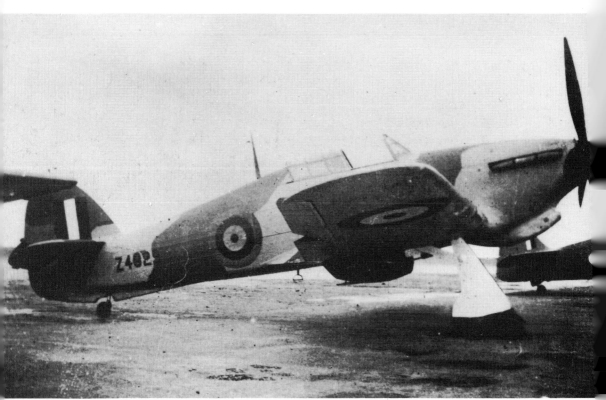

Left By 1941 many Hurricanes were serving in the Middle East. Z4929 shown here with tropical filter appeared to wear two-tone brown camouflage and azure blue under surfaces *(M.F.Genders)*.

Below left A formation of Dornier Do 17Zs believed to have been photographed during a 1940 daylight operation *(W.Skrzypczak)*.

Right The answer to the Dorniers — a flight of Spitfires of 64 Squadron taking off from Kenley during the Battle of Britian. 'SH:J' is nearest the camera *(contributor not named)*.

Right The Fairey Fulmar came into the news as the navy was supplying beleagured Malta. A Fulmar I is seen here, possibly aboard HMS *Illustrious (contributor not named)*.

Below One of KG 40's Condors, said to be an FW 200C-3/U1 and photographed on August 5 1942. It carries the identity number 0140 below the nose *(S.Hericzek)*.

Above Focke-Wulf Condors were rare over Britain — except for G-AGAY and that was far from common! There are no details of where and when the picture was taken, but it probably dates from 1941. The finish would then have been Dark Green-Dark Earth with silver under surfaces the black letters thereon having red-white-blue stripes below them. On the fuselage the letters were outlined silver *(Gavin Tyrrell)*.

Below Fulmar 1 '7F' gets away from a carrier in this 1941 shot *(J.E.Young)*.

Above The Beaufighter's good range was put to use quite early in its career when a number of Mk 1cs like T5043 were sent to the Middle East. The colours appear to be standard — two tones of brown with azure blue under surfaces, with a white letter, 'G', aft of the fuselage roundel *(D.W.Robinson)*.

Below It was in the Middle East that the Tomahawk saw most active service. No details of where or when this photograph was taken are known *(M.J.Allen)*.

Above left Flying over Jamaica in June 1942, Swordfish II W5858 carries a black 'A' outlined white on its fin *(F.G.Martin)*.

Left Swordfish 'L' misses the arrestor wires on HMS *Attacker* off Arran in 1942 *(F.G.Martin)*.

Above Swordfish II 'C' of 837 Squadron over Kingston, Jamaica, in July 1942 *(F.G.Martin)*.

Right Swordfish 'C' of 837 Squadron not long after. It crashed whilst landing on HMS *Dasher* in July 1942 *(F.G.Martin)*.

Left An early photograph of a Royal Navy Sikorski Hoverfly 1, with 'C' on the nose, bringing an Admiral aboard a carrier at Scapa Flow in 1945 *(F.G.Martin)*.

Below left There must be a most interesting story behind this photograph, which shows a Whitley VII of Coastal Command complete with the then very secret ASV radar under German guard *(contributor not named)*.

Bottom left A wartime shot of a Harvard II, AJ778 *(M.F.Genders)*.

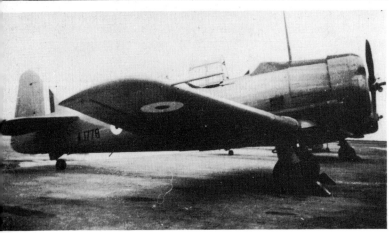

Above right A Goodyear blimp of the US Navy on patrol off New York in August 1942 *(F.G.Martin)*.

Right Wings locking into place on Avenger II, JZ472, on the deck of HMS *Queen* in 1944. The white lower surfaces were typical of some naval aircraft used for ocean patrol at that time *(F.G.Martin)*.

Left One of the first C-47s of the USAAF to visit Egypt. From the tone of the photograph this C-47 would appear to have the 'brown/grey' finish intended for such aircraft in the Middle East, yet often carried by them during their service in Britain. De Havilland Hornet Moth SU-ABT can be seen in the distance *(M.J.Allen)*.

Below left Avro Ansons used for communications purposes in the Middle East came into line with other aircraft in that theatre by having two-tone brown upper and blue lower surfaces. DG956, a Mk 1, is shown here *(M.J.Allen)*.

Below The engine cowling of the Polikarpov I-15 was very large, as can be seen in this picture of one of these Russian biplanes being inspected by Germans *(S.Herniczek)*.

Right Heinkel He 111s of KG 26 during a training flight over Denmark in the winter of 1941 *(S.Herniczek)*.

Below right 'Come on Wolfgang, give us a tune. But *please*, not "Lilli Marlene" again.' Alternatively, this might show a concert party entertaining a Heinkel 111 *(Witold Skrzypczak)*.

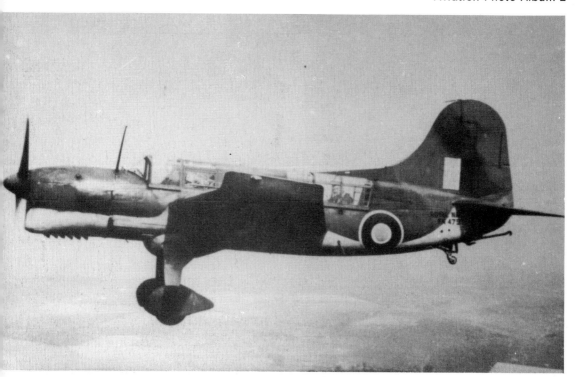

Above Only a few Curtiss Seamews ever reached the Royal Navy, although several hundreds were originally earmarked. Flying here is one of the earliest examples, FN475. The aircraft was finished in Dark Slate Grey and Extra Dark Sea Grey with Sky under surfaces. Note that the spats wear upper surface colours *(contributor not named)*.

Left Close-up of the nose of a Ju 88A carrying a 250 kg bomb *(contributor not named)*.

Below left Part of a line-up of Spitfire Vc (Tropical) fighters in use for operational training at No 73 OTU, Abu Sueir. Nearest is No 33, the serial number of which appears in four-inch digits and is JL306 *(M.Harries)*.

Above right One of those types of aeroplane that seems to have been around for ever. It is a Russian Polikarpov U-2 float-plane, registration CCCP- A1283 *(contributor not named)*.

Right A couple of early Seafires aboard an escort carrier. The forward one wearing a white letter 'B' has the serial number '. . 342' *(G.Neal)*.

Left The nose and tail unit of this Bell P-39N Airacobra — which carries the fin serial 218799 — appear to have been white like the number '247' on the nose. The photograph was taken on Guadalcanal *(J.I. McDonald)*.

Left One of the companions for the P-39 was this P-38G Lightning named 'Willie' and bearing '224' in white on its nose *(J.I.McDonald)*.

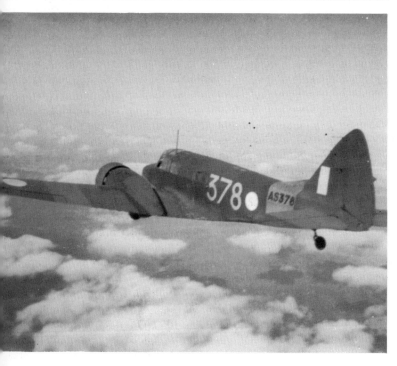

Left Certainly, it's an Oxford. It is flying over Southern Rhodesia, yet it is certainly wearing SEAC style roundels and fin flash. The number '378' appears to have been light grey, and a yellow band seems to surround the rear fuselage and carries the serial number AS378. There is another band around the mainplane. When one considers the large number of Oxfords built, it is amazing that so few photographs of them survive *(via M.J.F.Bowyer)*.

Right To have seen an Me 323 must have been one of life's great moments. It had a 180-foot wingspan and six engines and flew so slowly that one could enjoy the spectacle for some moments. What a thrill to have been actually piloting RF + XM. Do Me 323 pilots ever think about their memoirs? *(F.Richmond).*

Right In an idyllic Pacific setting, a Chance Vought F4U-1D Corsair of the RNZAF's No 14 Squadron *(E.C.V.Butler).*

OVERLEAF

Background photograph Production of the Boeing B-17C Flying Fortress totalled 38 aircraft, 20 of which saw service with the RAF. Three US Army Air Corps B-17Cs are seen here *(Boeing).*

Inset By a hangar at Kimbolton, B-17G 230298 'Busy Baby' of the 379th Bomb Group. The fuselage national insignia appears to have been overpainted in grey *(USAF photograph).*

Above In winter white, a Russian Yak-9. Apart from the red stars the only identity markings are painted in black on the fin and appear to be PO71/8371 *(contributor not named).*

Below Baltimores, possibly of 55 Squadron, flying over Italy. Details unknown *(P.F. Husband).*

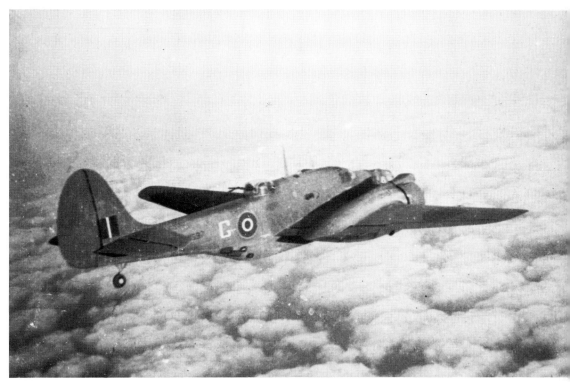

Above Lonely above the clouds, Baltimore IV FA537 'G' of No 15 Squadron, SAAF, flying over Italy in 1944. Desert camouflage is retained, and the aircraft letter is white *(Captain I.E.Peddle)*.

Below Another Baltimore IV, this time FA633 'T' and also of No 15 Squadron, SAAF, and again flying over Italy in 1944. This interesting photograph shows the Baltimore in a maritime reconnaissance role complete with white sides and under surfaces, and also with full ASV radar aerial array beneath the wings and nose *(Captain I.E.Peddle)*.

Above Little Snoring in the long shadows of deep winter of 1944/45. Mosquitoes of 515 Squadron of 100 Group stand dispersed with PZ383 in the foreground and wearing black and white belly stripes. A solitary swastika has been applied to the nose. The aircraft served with the squadron between August 1944 and July 1945 *(via M.G.Williams)*.

Below Lockheed Hudsons of the RNZAF — yes. But where and when remains unknown *(J.Lumley)*.

Above Grumman Avenger FN943 '4L' drones its way over some most inhospitable terrain *(contributor not named)*.

Below Impressive indeed. A close-up of the nose of a Junkers Ju 290 maritime reconnaissance aircraft. It is believed to have been in the hands of Fern-Aufklärungsgruppe 5 *(W. Skrzypczak)*.

Left In a jungle setting of Paya Lebar, a Kawasaki Army 99 'Lily' light bomber *(M.Mugridge)*.

Below left Stirling III EX-T:EE948 in an unusual pose. It was involved in an accident late in 1943 when with 199 Squadron. After repair it served with 1332 Conversion Unit *(Frank F. Smith)*.

Bottom left Possibly in a Balkan setting, this FW 190A-6 (Trop) wears a Gruppe Adjutant's chevron and II Gruppe bar. It is probably a 1944 photograph *(Neil Robinson)*.

Above right Two Firefly FR 1s with radomes painted out in the photograph. They are flying over HMS *Glory* passing through the Suva Straits. '279/Y' carries the serial number MB552 *(Kevin Marshal)*.

Right Pity this clear shot of a Lancaster gives no clue to its identity. The aircraft merely carries 'J' aft of the roundel, and could conceivably be from BDU Newmarket. Or — has it yet to acquire squadron letters? *(Alan Green)*.

Left NZ4047, a Catalina IV of the RNZAF *(N.Leicester)*.

Below left A close up of the nose of FW880 shows 29 bombs painted upon it *(contributor not named)*.

Below Three Baltimores, with Mk V FW880 'T' nearest. This was the last Baltimore produced for the RAF *(contributor not named)*.

Right I spied through my porthole, and what did I see? Three Cansos alighting most beautifully for me *(K.Morris)*.

Below right 'But Dad, you must come and look!' NZ4047, this time trying to hide its nose identity, KN-B *(N.Leicester)*.

Above A very appealing photograph of a Halifax III, LW179 of 102 Squadron. The aircraft was actually DY-E, but someone has doctored the print to show DY-D for the collection of a crew member who flew in D-Dog *(Eric L. Davies)*.

Left At first glance one would probably not identify this as a Lancaster, because it has the late war Rose-Rice turret which mounted .50 in calibre guns. A careful look shows something even more exotic, the aircraft was of 101 Squadron hence the ABC and other aerials *(Neil Robinson)*.

Above A Firefly FR 1 of 837 Squadron taxies in at Nowra, New South Wales *(David Reid)*.

Right Royal Navy Corsairs, said to be of 1831 Squadron during Far East deployment *(David Reid)*.

Left B-29 Superfortress 'Raz'n Hell' photographed on Okinawa *(contributor not named)*.

Below left The versatile Grumman Hellcat, actually seen here in postwar service with VF-695 of NAS Columbus, Ohio, in 1965 *(F.A.Bardshar)*.

Above right Also bearing American markings, but a very rare bird. An FW 190, sub-type uncertain, photographed in Germany in American hands. The fuselage has '... CFE' in black and a '5' can be seen on the undercarriage fairing. A Ju 188 is alongside. The photo was taken at Deldesdorf — anyone add any more? *(J.R.Kurrle)*.

Centre right A very rare shot of a Hotspur III. Note the strengthening struts on the tail unit, added to allow intensive flying. The black letters on the yellow fuselage rectangle, FEJJ, proclaim it as from No 3 Glider Training School. Absence of any yellow areas on the wings is interesting. The serial number begins with BT ...

Right FR209 became quite an anachronism, far outliving any other RAF Mitchell. After Boscombe Down trials July 1943 to April 1944, it passed to the Empire Central Flying School at Hullavington in September 1944, staying until October 1946. In August 1949 it joined the Meteorological Research Unit and was at Farnborough from September 1949 until May 1951. In September 1951 it became 6891M and was placed at Dyce. Hullavington, March 1949. Photos by R.J. Burgess.

Left What a sight! It appears to be a Mistel 2, but it is not the one that was shown at Farnborough in 1945. Both aircraft have AIR MIN numbers but they are not readable. Behind squats a Ju 52 *(G.M.Hodgson)*.

Below left A captured Bf 110 displaying the curious style of roundel applied to some of such aircraft *(M.J.Larsen)*.

Above A very unusual sight at Kimbolton: a B-17E photographed on July 24 1944. One was accustomed to seeing striped, gaily painted B-24s, but not B-17s. The code letters are FR. In its halcyon days 'Birmingham Blitzkrieg' had been a pioneer of the 8th Air Force, but the white stripes on the drab finish depicted here show it in target towing garb *(USAF photograph)*.

Below Burtonwood on March 10 1944 with B-24s lined up awaiting active service, a US Navy Liberator side on and, surprise, surprise, 19112, an old B-17E with fascinating nose and tail gun turrets *(USAF photograph)*.

Overflying *Ark Royal*'s deck, a Gannet AEW 3 '430' of 849 Squadron *(G. Wyatt)*.

POST 1945 PERIOD

Left When the war ended the Fairchild Argus abruptly disappeared from British skies when the Air Transport was quickly disbanded. Many Arguses were disposed of overseas, a few to British civil operators. But abroad the RAF made some use of them as communications aircraft. FS617 seen here in silver finish, a Mk II, carries black serial numbers and was photographed at its base, Fayid *(Alan Green)*.

Below left Very aggressive looking aeroplane, the Tempest II *(Alan Thomas)*.

Above right Another view of Tempest IIs of 5 Squadron at Poona. Nearest is PR720:A, then PR623:B and PR536:R *(Alan Thomas)*.

Right Sunderland GRV WQ-T of 209 Squadron beached at Seletar. The nose bears the squadron badge *(contributor not named)*.

Below Dutch Mitchells lined up on Kemajoran, Batavia. Note the bar national insignia. N5.233 is nearest, next N5.245. Beyond are RAF Thunderbolts whose code letters appear to be a tantalising '?J' *(contributor not named)*.

Above left Surely one of the most impressive piston-engined fighters, the de Havilland Hornet. PX228 had the high altitude grey/blue finish *(Alan Green)*.

Left Another view of PX228. Interesting in that it had provision for wing drop tanks. It was sent overseas for weathering trials and on return was disected at Hatfield to assess its weathering qualities *(Alan Green)*.

Above SR919, the final production Beaufighter, converted to TT 10 standard. Finish is silver with yellow and black striped under surfaces. Photographed at Hullavington in March 1949 by R.J.Burgess.

Below A Martin P4M Mercator, an immediate post-war patrol bomber which in this photograph can be seen to have been much decorated with radomes containing electronic gear for the collection of radio intelligence material. The nose carries '6' in white, the tail 'JQ' *(Chris Wilson)*.

Above left Only limited use was made of the Stirling V as a civil transport despite high hopes. OO-XAS is seen here, silver with black letters *(R.Staton)*.

Left When C-74 Globemasters began regular flights to Europe in 1948 they were the largest USAF aircraft then in regular service. CN-414, serial number 42-65414, seen here was photographed on September 15 1948 during the Berlin Air Lift *(Carl Brooks)*.

Below left Companion on the air lift, an Avro York of 51 Squadron photographed in 1948 *(Carl Brooks)*.

Above York MW165 unloads at Gatow, with a Halton behind *(Carl Brooks)*.

Right Dakota IV KN477 with the letters 'KJ' on a black panel ahead of the fuselage roundel makes its way over Egypt *(Peter Simms)*.

Above Photographed not long before the withdrawal of the Sunderland V in the Far East is 'U' of 205/209 Squadron afloat off Seletar *(D.M.Stanley)*.

Below Sunderlands always looked particularly attractive when seen head on — but then flying-boats looked attractive from all angles! *(D.M.Stanley)*.

Above Brough, 1949, and a Blackburn Firecrest rests on jacks to permit undercarriage retraction tests. JATO bottles may be seen in the foreground *(R.V.K.Jackson)*.

Below Miles Marathons of No 1 ANS. 'Q' is XA267 and 'L' just visible is XA258. Both are silver with yellow 'T bands' and black lettering *(D.L.Jackson)*.

Above Sabre F 1 XB578:C of 234 Squadron at Geilenkirchen in 1955 *(A.Jones)*.

Below What a superb setting. A Canberra B 6 of 100 Squadron photographed on Christmas Island *(contributor not named)*.

Above An early production Meteor T 7, VW418 in silver finish with yellow bands at Hullavington in March 1949 *(R.J.Burgess).*

Below Sea Hawk 1s of 804 Squadron including WF207 lined up at Brawdy whilst a Dragonfly passes with a cyclist in tow *(G.Wyatt).*

How about this then — and what a backdrop! Rapide ZK-AKY was photographed in May 1969 at Queenstown, Otago. It was one of four used by New Zealand Tourist Air Travel for scenic flights over South Island. On the silver finish the cheat lines were red. The aircraft's upper surfaces were cream *(J.Hinton)*.

Above left An Attacker F 1, WA474 '113' of 736 Squadron *(G.Wyatt)*.

Left Three Meteor F 8s of No 1 Squadron *(B.Cox)*.

Above Dakota 4 12968 of No 429 Squadron, Canadian Armed Forces, photographed at Downsview, Ontario, on September 1 1973. Finish is silver with white top and red cheat line *(B.T.Gibbins)*.

Above right The Reid & Sigrist RS 4 Bobsleigh VZ728 at Desford on June 13 1951. The machine, previously G-AGOS, has been fitted up for prone pilot use. It is currently housed at Strathallan. Here it is in silver finish *(R.Staton)*.

Right Meteor III EE401 in standard grey-green finish *(M.Schoeman)*.

Above There are not all that many Harvards left in Europe now. The example seen here, D-FDOK, was used for skywriting *(J.L.McDonald)*.

Below Many air forces found a use for the noisy Harvard. One was the South African AF, one of whose machines, 7710, is seen at Rand in the mid-1950s. It is believed to have been in the hands of the Central Flying School *(D.Becker)*.

Above Boeing-Vertol CH-113 Voyageur 11311 of 450 Squadron, Canadian Armed Forces, based at Ottawa South (Uplands Airport) and photographed at Downsview on September 1 1973 *(B.T.Gibbins)*.

Below Lined up at Tengah in 1969 — Sabres of No 77 Squadron, Royal Australian Air Force. A94-970 nearest has a white '70' on its nose and on the fin checks carries the squadron's black horse head emblem, repeated with '77' on the long-range tank feature *(contributor not named)*.

Above Super Frelon '12' of the Aeronavale cruises off the French west coast (F. Richmond).

Above left 'Come in', they said, so I did. 'Yes, take as many pictures as you like — before we shoot you.' So I did. This is a close-up of the nose of a Tu-16. The long serial number 4200601 is to make such things harder to collect (Wieslaw).

Left The tail unit of 4200601, with '72' at the tip (Wieslaw).

Right This further close-up of a Tu-16 appears to be of 1881301. The dispersal pens seem to be of most primitive style *(Wieslaw)*.

Below right Supermarine Attackers of 736 Squadron. WA531 nearest, numbered 152, has a red nose tip, and is an FB Mk 1 *(G.Wyatt)*.

Below WP299, an Attacker FB Mk 2 109/LM, was also in the hands of 736 Squadron at Lossiemouth when this photograph was taken *(G.Wyatt)*.

Above left Interesting in that this is an early Seahawk Mk 6 which first flew on February 18 1955. It is XE339 and carries the markings of 803 Squadron which it wore in 1957 *(A.W.Feist)*.

Left In midnight blue finish, Skyraider WT965 of 849 Squadron about to settle on the deck of HMS *Eagle (A.W.Feist)*.

Above Certainly a panorama from the past. Neptunes from Kinloss pass over Sea Hornet 20s and Seahawks at the 1954 Lossiemouth open day *(G.Wyatt)*.

Above right Meteor NF 11 WM187 of 151 Squadron wears a black 'G' on its fin. Photographed at Shawbury in 1953 *(R.Jones)*.

Right If foreign air forces interest you, then at once you will know this is a Columbian Air Force Beechcraft T-34 Mentor *(F.Richmond)*.

The Post 1945 Period

Left The Bell UH-1B Iroquois seen here is also of the Columbian Air Force *(F. Richmond)*.

Right To complete the Columbian trio — Lockheed C-130 Hercules FAC 1001 *(F. Richmond)*.

Below left A delightful memory of an era passed. Gannet AEW 3, XL494 of 849 Squadron's 'C' Flight, is on *Ark Royal*'s steam catapult awaiting launch while a Whirlwind offers plane guard *(G.Wyatt)*.

Right Rarely seen in the skies of Great Britain, a Shackleton 2 of 205 Squadron, WL795, flying over Gan in September 1968 *(contributor not named)*.

Below Companion to the Shackleton, a Breguet Atlantic of the Aeronavale *(F. Richmond)*.

Above left A very clear flying shot of a CM 170 Magister of the French Air Force *(F.Richmond)*.

Left Two Sea Vixen FAW 1s of 890 Squadron indulge in air-to-air refuelling. XN649 leads, XJ584 trails *(G. Wyatt)*.

Above Short Stirling Mk V transports of No 1589 Heavy Freight Flight. 'KA' PJ994 nearest has grey-green upper camouflage and Azure Blue under surfaces. PJ975 is silver overall. They were photographed at Fanara in the Canal Zone, Egypt, in June 1946 *(P.Rowland)*.

Above right The French ancestry of this Super Frelon is evident in the tail legend SA 321L No 139. The helicopter, '313', is in the hands of No 15 Squadron, SAAF, and was based at Swartkop when the picture was taken at Potchedfshoom *(D.Becker)*.

Right A C 160Z Transall '331' of 28 Squadron, SAAF, based at Waterkloof. Finish is overall natural metal but with a white fuselage top *(D.Becker)*.

Above Fiesler Fi 156 Storch VX154 was brought to Britain after the war for evaluation *(T.W.Yates)*.

Left After the war the French Air Force made use of a number of Ju 52 3/M variants, two of which can be seen here *(T.W.Yates)*.

Left Three Avro Yorks lined up by hangar at Odiham, and believed to be of 51 Squadron. PE106 is nearest *(T.W.Yates)*.

Right Oxford HM760, an all-silver example, was in the hands of Odiham's Station Flight when this photgraph was taken *(T.W.Yates)*.

Right For many years the Swedish Air Force used Ju 86s as transports to support overseas visits by their aircraft. Three Ju 86s here gave support to a visit to Britain by P-51 Mustangs *(T.W.Yates)*.

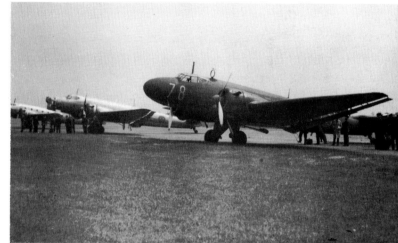

Below Three Vampire F 3s of 54 Squadron taking off from Odiham, with VT869 in the lead *(T.W.Yates)*.

Above One of the first USAF jet fighters to call in on Britain, Lockheed P-80A-LO 485464, on the way to Furstenfeldbruck in July 1948. The nose is red and red bands flank the yellow areas on the tip tanks and around the fuselage *(T.W.Yates)*.

Below Although the nose designation proclaims a B-29, this aircraft was really an F-13, photo version of the Superfortress. FG-583:461583 named 'KAMRA-KAZE' was used for photography during the Bikini atomic bomb trials *(T.W.Yates)*.

Bottom F-80 Shooting Stars lined up at Odiham in 1948 *(T.W.Yates)*.